MW00776638

DISTANCE

WITHOUT

DISTANCE

BY THE SAME AUTHOR:

Color
(Membrane, 1976)

Disappearing Work
(The Figures, 1979)

Robinson Crusoe: A New Fiction
(Membrane, 1983)

Life Moves Outside
(Burning Deck, 1987)

Eva and the Bluebird
(Five Fingers Press chapbook, 1993)

DISTANCE

WITHOUT

DISTANCE

BARBARA EINZIG

KELSEY ST. PRESS

Some of these works first appeared in *Conjunctions, o-blek, Pequod, St. Mark's Newsletter, Talisman, Tyuonyi, Voice Literary Supplement,* and *Writing.*

I wish to acknowledge the support of the Tisch School of the Arts at New York University, the Literature Department of the University of California at San Diego, and the New York Foundation for the Arts.

Space in which to work was provided by Andy and Helen Norman of Palisades, New York, in the summer and fall of 1989, and in the spring of 1990 by the Centro de Estudios Latinoamericanos Romulo Gallegos in Caracas, Venezuela.

Heartfelt thanks to all of the above.

.

Publication of this book was made possible in part by grants from the National Endowment for the Arts, the California Arts Council, and the LEF Foundation.

Copyright © 1994 Barbara Einzig

Cover: *Untitled* by Vija Celmins, 1986–87, oil on canvas
Collection of Donna O'Neill, Los Angeles. Courtesy McKee Gallery, New York.
(Photo: Sheldan Collins)

Library of Congress Cataloging-in-Publication Data

Einzig, Barbara.
    Distance without distance / Barbara Einzig.
        p.   cm.
    ISBN 0-932716-34-2
    I. Title.
    PS3555.I6D57   1994
    813'.54 — dc20   94–12381
                                                        CIP

Book design and production by Lory Poulson. Text: Trump Medieval.
Printed by West Coast Print Center, Berkeley. Paper: Carnival.

Kelsey St. Press, 2718 Ninth Street, Berkeley, California 94710 (510-845-2260)

Distributed by Small Press Distribution (800-869-7553)
and Inland Books (800-243-0138)

for Chloe

.

and for my mother and father

CONTENTS

And if, upon waking, we hastily and
greedily take possession of the night's
adventures as if they belonged to us,
do we not do so with a certain sense
of usurpation (as well as gratitude),
do we not carry with us the memory of
an irreducible distance, a peculiar sort
of distance, a distance between self and
self, but also a distance between all the
characters and the various identities
(however certain) we confer on them,
a distance without distance, illuminating
and fascinating, somewhat like nearing the
far-off or making contact with remoteness?

— MAURICE BLANCHOT,

"DREAMING, WRITING"

Composition is in no essential an escape
from life.

— WILLIAM CARLOS WILLIAMS

The Miracle of Tenses

She remembered it as a time of intense feeling, the days when their child had just been born. The child's amazement at being born was fully coincident with the event; the mother had never seen such an expression as was on her face. For her face was not used to being a face, to being seen; she had never been seen before. She was not amazed at something but in something, so she was not amazed at all, but was herself amazement. Then the baby slept, and the father slept, and she lay awake between them, because the baby had promised for so long to come that she must be prepared for waiting and then it was here. We are all here in the world where we are, but it had been somewhere else, and before that it had not been, so that despite the fact that we all have arrived here by being born, there is nothing more common, the event of the child's birth, the child's existence, was extraordinary, a paradox that did not escape her.

It was November, and the day of the naming ceremony it snowed. It was all white outside and the room was full of flowers. The snow did not last long, but melted cleanly in the strong sun, leaving no trace. Awake the baby with her large dark eyes looked out the window and made graceful falling motions with her fists, remembering through these gestures where she had been and what she had been doing just before being born, but without thinking of that place or action as we do. The movements remembered themselves, they repeated themselves but now had space in which to fall and so, startling, they gradually forgot themselves and changed to open hands that learned to touch and hold.

Remembering this time puts it in the past, and it has been long enough ago now to want to do so, we want to live in the present moment. It hadn't been easy, and it seemed she couldn't just take or leave anything anymore, but had to worry about it and take care of it. Chains of tiny actions must be sustained: while being dressed, one hand keeps the baby from rolling off the changing table while the other dabs a washcloth into the warm water of a small bowl. Layers of clothing are resisted and go on with effort; all this must have been washed and prepared, in the middle knocked over, washed and soiled, it is washed and prepared and set out or put on again. At last they go out into the winter sunlight. While the leaves had been falling the baby had been crying for her attention or squirming against her chest and even when it was asleep she was held to it in fascination. So when she looked up into the sky for the first time in a long time she saw the branches of sycamores and elms revealed — a gray, white, chalky brown.

Dark spots suspended among them were the nests of birds, and a squirrel ran easily out to where the branch thinned and bent under its nimble weight which, practiced, used this giving way as a springboard to the neighboring tree. The cool air makes the colors brittle, or the gold leaves are suddenly wasted, trunks further lined with shadows dark and defined where the branches that throw them are close by or soft shadows where the light is blocked further away.

The days turned into weeks that they counted its age by.

Remembering it put it in the past, though the power of the event continued to live in the form of the child and its life.

Is part of being in a new love remembering acts of this new love? And why does this remembering not put the act of love safely in the past but cause us to relive it as if it were a blood infusing us?

"Friendship Is No Less a Mystery than Love"

(BORGES)

When morning begins, certain small animals are seen to be moving, directly, a formation of birds in the sky, or by inference, a flower that falls, dislodged by a moving weight, lizard, iguana, squirrel. Precedent. This is a movement that started before its sighting, when it was still dark, Mexico, a black bird unfolding white wings, a new name unknown or hard to pronounce, flying low over the farm of prickly pear whose fruits, about to ripen, are green, the color of forests.

And in the northern one the white wings really flashed there, seagulls, clean pines mixed with redwoods, a density close to water, as I am not of their kind I do not pretend to know their habits. Witness. That is, their moving has an environment surrounding it, and this, as we know it, is not human.

As we know it, human, and dressed for purposes of sport, his arms reach down, hands touch the podium. Says. So I am not in these woods, and the birds began their flight before I knew them with my eyes. The words go back to what was held in their flight. Repetition, rhythm, the sound of branches cracking as a sign.

The air will be moved by a structure of bones and feathers that is alive. Foreign language. And they move on the ground, too, and from the windows of a bus going toward the pyramids. A mix of tenses. The one on the sidewalk clicks his fingers and makes a gesture suggestive of a knife, a proposition, integrates this white wing. Your move.

Puzzling out his speech, her own pattern of understanding (her native tongue) came into evidence as they heaved and cracked.

A large hill of powdered brick and in the same red but
clear, enameled, and still wet

PINTURAS DUPONT

corroded

information of the landscape. The bus is headed back from the pyramids for Mexico City, past the rows of pines painted white to waist-high.

After Christoph Hein's *The Distant Lover*

We come to know the daily life of Claudia, a woman in East Berlin, without ever learning her last name. It doesn't matter — she could be anyone. She's a doctor, but there's nothing spectacular about her practice, made up of the usual variety of ailments, minor complaints, loneliness. She's divorced from another doctor, also not unusual, and lives in an apartment building where the tenants change frequently. *It's not worth getting to know anyone.*

.

It's told in her own voice, made up of observations. The distant lover is Henry Sommer, whose last name is given at his own funeral, in the opening chapter. It's said to Claudia at the cemetery, to make sure that everyone present is at the right funeral, since several are happening at the same time. To learn it at that moment makes him seem not better known, but more anonymous, not unusual.

.

Claudia works, visits with family and friends (she has no children), goes on vacation. On short forays into the green countryside, she photographs landscapes and buildings that are either abandoned, no longer serving their old purposes, or are in a state of disrepair, falling into decay, a suggestion of nature. Periodically she develops batches of these shots herself, turning her kitchen into a lab, but never exhibits and has no desire to do so, considering them nothing spectacular.

.

From Henry's funeral backward, the book chronicles Claudia's knowing him, over a year's time. Nothing spectacular happens between them. They both keep people at arm's length and appear unmoved by the things around them. Nevertheless, everything is tracked exactly, as if it were important.

The officer from Frau Rupprecht's apartment was standing between the two elevator doors, pressing both call buttons. He too had a coat over his arm, a sort of military raincape. Maybe he was with the police and not the army. I can't tell all their uniforms apart. A bag stuck out from under his cape, some kind of attaché case. He nodded to me when I approached. Then without a word turned back to the elevator buttons. He kept tapping out a rhythm with the toe of his boot.

Claudia doesn't miss anything, although the clues don't add up to something, as they would in a detective story, but only suggest the shape of an uncertainty, a lack of knowledge of other people's lives.

Henry jumps into her bed and sleeps with her. That's how it starts between them. Fond of each other, they are similar in nature, sharing a conviction that intimacy is false. Each holds this view a little differently. He keeps the past away from him, having no use for it, drives fast and banks on chance to save him from disaster. The intensity makes him feel alive.

She is careful to avoid what some might call human connection, the rituals arising from things done by people over and over, an *established familiarity*. On call she often sees bad accidents and attends to the survivors. Even when she's not working, people turn to her for help and she gives it, kindness, although she despises her "doctor voice," *the mask of our helplessness.*

•

Mother said she was having a very hard time with him; as she said this, she stroked my hand. I didn't know how to respond. It seemed strange that she expected me to comfort her. This was something she'd have to get through on her own. Besides, if I touched her, she would just start crying again.

•

While I was reading it, I was thinking of something else, not unusual. But I was not distracted. The book had evoked these thoughts, brought them out of hiding, the flute the children followed. Several may be happening at the same time, thoughts accompanying things that happen as a kind of music. The distinction between thinking and dreaming may be exaggerated.

.

Before I went to bed, I kissed my mother goodnight. No, I got up out of bed to kiss her goodnight, saying that I had almost forgotten. She smiled as if I was fooling her, playing tricks to stay awake, and after I kissed her, putting my arms around her neck and pulling her to me, said with a smile and knowingly that I didn't have to kiss her every night. Someday I wouldn't kiss her goodnight at all, and I would have forgotten all about it. It confused me the way she said it, as if it were something that had already happened. I told her no, I would always kiss her before I went to bed, always, every night, and that I wasn't going to forget. My voice as I said this confused me, sounding as if I were angry. I wasn't angry, but something in my voice sounded angry, as if it were agreeing with her description of what was going to happen when I grew up.

It begins with a dream of walking on a broken bridge over a bottomless abyss.

For the first three or four steps we cling to the railing. Then it ends, splintered, jagged, thrusting into the air, a severed torso.

The severed torso occurs that way, red and yellow.

Something can be a suggestion of itself, and can keep suggesting itself until it becomes that thing.

A lack of courage could be that way.

Something can take on momentarily the properties of another thing.

It does not really look like this other thing. It's clearly the railing of a bridge. It suggests a severed torso by taking on the properties of that thing, which was once a person, but now is only part of a person.

The frog looked just like a leaf, and not any kind of leaf, but just the kind it had fallen among, in an identical stage of decay. Although now all red and yellow and brown, it must have been recently green, for it was not yet dried out but firm, the way leaves still on trees are.

But the frog hadn't fallen but jumped there, with its compact, springy body. It only looked like it had fallen — it was hiding. Even its outline, which of course it couldn't lose, was kept from standing out through a resemblance to the veins of leaves, lines not around things but among them, a concealed dimension. Its body, once recognized, was complicated. But the sharp, small features, angles, could pretend to be lines, a network of veins in a mass of decaying leaves.

I couldn't have seen it on my own. The little girl pointed it out to me with its name, pointing with her lips and laughing, while her older sister pushed me to the side so I wouldn't step on it. The push startled me, not because it was rough but so quick and definite, the way one flexes back the branch of a tree that gets in the way, and happening as I saw the frog. Right then I didn't feel like a person, or the way I'd imagined persons feel, but like part of the woods, when she pushed me that way.

Somewhere in the depths of the elevator shaft came a rustling, a vibration of steel cables, the promise of a change long wished for, the sort of hope that fosters patience.

.

Perhaps she gives the small kindnesses out of an old, almost involuntary part of herself, a part of a person in hiding, that wants to love again as she loved her childhood friend, Katharina, a religious person in an atheist state and the only student who refuses to join the socialist youth organization. Growing up for Claudia is learning to keep quiet. She loses Katharina by turning on her through a lack of courage, the herd instinct, the fear of standing out.

.

Nonetheless a reassuring presence within the nameless, inexplicable entity that is also me.

The frog was only pointed out because I was about to step on it. Briefly this amused my companions while we kept moving on, away from the clear yellow river we'd just crossed (on logs I could finally dart over), to the gardens we would work.

The frog's name said laughingly was of course its Yekuana one. It probably doesn't have another one, but it might, yes it must have a Yanomami or a Pemon or a Penare one. But it probably doesn't have one in our language because it doesn't exist here.

I remember the name only as a quick high sound, two or three as she laughed and said it, the way one says the name of a child old enough to recognize its name being called, without having to answer.

It knew we'd found it, but all its effort was absorbed in suppressing its breathing, slowing down its small heart, so big in the body that could have disappeared were it not betrayed by its beating.

The other beam trembles after the runners have crossed, and then grows still. We could go on. Or maybe we should turn back. But for us there is no turning back; we have to cross. And now it is even more hopeless.

The experience occurs at exactly that speed, not an "experience" but something unknown that is occurring in our presence. Or, it is happening to us, so we have a chance to know it. Clearly it has an independent life, whether or not it is known or seen or remembered.

The dream can't be speeded up or it would change. Some of the things that happened (her being frightened at the distinctness of the runners' faces, the lack of sound) would not happen in the telling of it, and would be lost. This happens all the time, as things are not remembered.

When she returns to a town where she lived in her childhood, she finds some of the same people and brick buildings, but not what she is looking for. As she has almost forgotten the girl she was, the town has forgotten itself.

I — or this person who may be me — hesitate.

Are these words mine or the author's? I can find them in the book, longing to be released from themselves, to lose themselves in a murmur of voices, the waves and crescendos of the insects in the summer trees.

I dreamt at night but I also dreamt during the day. This dreaming was like a music accompanying the several things that would happen to me each day. To say that I was successful and powerful in these dreams would hopelessly blur the delicate, distinct pleasure found there. There I wrote something that was beautiful; I sang in a voice impersonal as sex and as miraculous. A fuzzy kind of praise, anonymous, enveloped me, just as petting would in my later adolescence when as a boy felt my breasts I would almost fall asleep, not out of boredom but as a means of losing inhibition, a kind of trance, like getting mildly drunk.

.

She does not have an easy time sleeping.

.

She washes her body thoroughly the first time she is kissed, and also does so after she takes care of the birds of the woman next door who has died.

Quotation marks are never used when a person is speaking. Claudia just tells us what they said. Although it might be exact, sometimes it is just a part of what was said, or what she remembers. (Even in one's native language, everything isn't understood, although this pretense is maintained, concealing dimension. When speaking another language, it can be dispensed with.) So we are forced to share her fate, which is not to get outside of herself.

•

At home I would wrap everything and go through my address book, which was cluttered with little pencil checks next to the names. Names of people from all the past Christmases for whom I'd tortured my brain thinking up so-called personal gifts. Today I no longer even look for personal gifts, anything will do. Besides, I don't know what a personal gift is. I think if I really gave someone a personal gift, it would scare him to death. I don't know what a personal gift for myself would be, either. But I'm sure that if it were really personal, I would burst into tears. At least I'd know then what sort of person I am.

•

He said that he also felt that he stood out at home, so that here, in a foreign country, it was a relief to be endowed with this status as an objective and unchangeable fact. He explained that not fitting in didn't weigh on him here, sounding as if he were happy.

•

Henry's irony makes him so distant that, in the end, it's almost as if he were pretending to be in a fight, except that it kills him.

•

From the time that she turned on her friend, her perceptions began to change. Not only details are no longer telling; undeniably important events are dulled to prohibit the reaction that might endanger oneself (as if we are in hiding).

We stood with the crowd on the sidewalk and looked at the tank. Nothing was happening. People whispered to one another. Later the tank's upper hatch opened and a young Russian soldier looked out. He didn't seem to be afraid. He nodded to us. . . . Things remained quiet, and I was getting bored. We went home.

•

She works to hide each thing from itself.

Boredom is created.

Things and people suggest within themselves other possibilities of what they could be. They are not these possibilities, yet these suggestions are now part of them. The narrator's voice shares properties with other sounds, impersonal as sex and as miraculous. Words share properties with other words. The music accompanying their activities is not distracting, although neither is it background music. Balanced, it establishes certain registers corresponding to green things found within the activities. Of course, these things are not themselves notes. Or they are notes, but notes that have not yet been sounded, or are sounded by the music accompanying them, which then awakes them to themselves (undoing her work), if they could be considered living things, or at least awakes them to ourselves, who hear names casually, often even forgetting them, having nothing but these activities for our companions.

After Wim Wenders' *Die angst des tormanns beim elfmeter*
(The Goalie's Anxiety at the Penalty Kick)

The apple in the film looks so good. Leaning forward, he is in focus, and the background of green countryside a blur. Since the film is in German with subtitles in Spanish, a language I'm learning, I have to think, and miss part of what happens.

He said that in Caracas foreigners are like Jews were in Poland. But that wasn't exactly what he said.

Fortunately for me, it employs a small vocabulary or has been translated simply, using clear constructions and basic words.

Approximations of men are drinking together, and soon they are fighting. It's raining, and the rain is like the background before, something that extends, cleans, or heals through its lack of definition, and the fight is like the man leaning forward in focus. Green hills, gray slashes of water, a background filling itself in or painting itself, a computer adding information of a third dimension through shading. But he is badly hurt and the rain washes over him where he has fallen. Someone helps him up.

He said that gradually as he got older he became more self-centered and spoke less of himself.

One pronounces the words silently, these subtitles. There are sudden amounts of music and shots of breezes expressed in thin, moving curtains.

I was thinking about the difference between "fragmented" and "broken."

It's the story of a man — the goalie of the title — who's murdered someone he barely knows. The police sketch is a good resemblance, yet we feel he won't be found out, for the intensity of his preoccupation with his crime serves him as a shield. He had this quality even before committing the crime, when he was leaning forward, against the blurred countryside. He had been careful to wipe his fingerprints off the coffee cup and to pick up his change from the tablecloth after he killed her, the woman who sold tickets to the movies.

We noticed his precise awareness of what he had touched of what was around him.

In the end, someone recognizes him while sitting next to him at a soccer match — the game he plays professionally.

Identification does not necessarily determine the story. It contributes. Vectors form bouquets, and the second image on the screen is that of a hand holding cards.

People in the business of guarding something make good characters.

Calibrations

1

It is not possible to write when one has an object.

Object in the sense of purpose, although they term the purpose of a story its subject.

The climate is one of a neutralized grammar.

This occurs when basic categories of one language find no direct correspondence in another.

Meaning?

It was too early in the morning for such a question. The canoes leave when the dark begins to, to make a good distance before the heat intensifies. The darkness and chill will part and lighten, and we find ourselves moving steadily forward in a cloud at dawn. Yellow day separates the water that is the cloud from the river water. Cutting through dense, towering rain-forest, the river's only horizon a thick point straight ahead, its turn.

2

I first heard a voice singing and wondered where it was. I went outside to wander closer to where it was, but could not approach it. Phenomenon of the horizon. Yet it was out there and trying to fall asleep I wondered not where but what it was, and I wondered at how I might know it.

This is the thirty-second time that this small bird has been captured today. It has pollen on its beak; it has been drinking from a flower. The other is tracked by radar. All day it stays close to the army ants, and at night it sleeps in the treetops above the anthill. In this way their habits are recorded.

The linguist Benjamin Whorf called these correspondences between languages calibrations. He found the place of meaning not in words and morphemes but in the patterned relations BETWEEN them, in their RAPPORT, the *processes and linkages of a NONMOTOR type, silent, invisible, and individually unobservable.*

A plot was originally a clearing in the woods. Poetry is a theater in which the natural forces that shift the meanings of words in times and contexts play. Both Whorf and the poet Velemir Khlebnikov called the basic units of language elements.

In the heat and silence my companions went in and out of humming. The motor had gone so there was the sound of the paddles, going into the water and leaving it. As they flew over, parrots squawked, sawing or tearing the air. The sky was now a strong pale blue and thin enormous clouds shape, move, and dissolve on the broadening horizon.

3

The woodpecker's sound rang out. Or a sound. Rang out. What made it.

He said that the documentation of the value of a particular species of plant, insect, or bird is dependent upon its disappearance, for its role in the life of the forest becomes clear through the effects of its absence.

This clearing is the beloved place of Zangezi. Here he comes every morning and recites his songs. Here he chants to the people, to the forest. A tall spruce, its blue needlewaves waving violently, stands straight, shuts away this part of the cliff, a friend guarding its peace.

This is also the place of Walter Benjamin's pure language, *where all information, all sense, and all intention finally encounter a stratum in which they are destined to be extinguished.* This pure language is released from one's own language in the act of translation, in poetic action. The object is extinguished as the subject, or referent, shifts and floats, fighting its placement.

After John Cage's *Europeras 1 & 2*

At the last minute I decided to go to the performance. It was at Pace, across the river, and I left while it was still light. On the phone charging the ticket the man gave me detailed directions on how to get there. Because I was going alone it felt like a pilgrimage, although the only time in my life I saw anyone going on one, they went together, a family.

They were before me, on a mountain path where I was traveling, the trade route between Nepal and Tibet. It is now more than ten years ago that I was there; the main things we saw carried were salt, bags of produce so assorted they must have come from gardens rather than farms, and bright Chinese tennis shoes. Everyone we saw was wearing these shoes, or was barefoot.

In the summer there is not much traffic on the Tappan Zee, and I quickly drove over. The bridge was built at the widest point — in more convenient places the land was too valuable. Even so, it destroyed some of the best homes in the village. I looked down as I went over, remembering how a few months ago Dennis was netting shad there.

He had told me to go up the hill, following the signs, which took me to a parking lot he said had never been filled. The cars had not wanted to line up beside each other as they arrived (too much like a herd), so they parked in different places, distributing themselves unevenly.

He had said the orchestra seats were oddly divided by price, and although he should not be saying so, I should move in toward the middle if there was space. The performance was a collage of operas unprotected by copyright, with arias, costumes, actions, et cetera, selected by chance. When I came back to this country everyone was wearing brown and black, but now very bright colors are in fashion, and they blossom in the audience before the scrim rises and the lights go down.

With the audience so engaged in the observation of lush spec-
tacle (he said in the sense of a circus, and not a series of climaxes),
thoughts entering the minds of the audience are oracular. The
subject never appears, the power behind the throne, the woman
behind the man.

Now that what we have inherited is gone
Now that what we have inherited has left us
        these props   that are alive
            and these animals   that have eyes

The path meandered along cliffs, winding up the mountain valley, now deforested, terraced to potatoes and yellow rape. Each time it wound outward, a false summit appeared on the horizon, a little hill that had the sky at the top. The one they now approached was steep; the steps carved into it were forced to nearly double back so as to mount it. She had on the bright striped woolen apron the married women wear there, and all her jewelry. Her boys were busy scrambling up in front of her, brown and naked except for dusty black pants held up with rope. The father brought up the rear, beating a drum as he walked. I had heard it before seeing them, when they were still over the next rise. In turning back he saw me and that I was about to take their picture, so he raised the drum's face in front of his own. The politeness of this refusal stunned me, the gesture performed so impersonally, as if it were not his but the drum's response to my camera, which I immediately lowered from in front of my face. Later I learned they had walked from another country and were on their way to a sacred lake, where they would briefly immerse themselves, fully clothed.

The audience knew that her dress represented a whole way of life that had disappeared, but they did not know what it was.

While I was missing something, they were entering and leaving the place, which being in front of an audience is called a stage. In a way, a sentence is the same. I must have been thinking or something, they must have come on in front of me without my noticing, for there are new props here. She is there, mysteriously enjoying emptying the pool with a small cup.

In New Guinea a few months ago the male bowerbirds were building arbors from branches and laying out blue, yellow-green, brown and gray things there — feathers, flowers, fruits, snailshells, mushrooms. He paints his construction with crushed purple fruit, or mixes charcoal in this paste to make a darker color. The brown gardener bird who lives deep in the forest decorated his circular house with orchids that go on living there. He too was spreading colored things around his garden. Sheep's vertebrae, bits of glass or porcelain, spoons, forks and coins, he placed upon his lush stage, where he was picking them up and dancing with each one to catch the sunlight and the female. Where there are opals, prospectors rob the collections as valuable concentrations; an armaments factory in these woods puts mesh on the windows to keep out these birds, who steal screws, bolts, and other small pieces for their plays.

If you are a horse you raise and lower your head in a certain way, and paw at the ground in   restlessness   anticipation something we do not know.

A beast of burden has no such freedom.

If one knows the aria, one knows where it comes from. They all used to know the stories they were in, for they lived in the same place for the greater part of their lives. They had all been told the same stories of the ancients, so that when they put on plays of them they already knew what they were about.

Because they were undefended it was easy to conquer them. On the other hand, they were able to retreat forever behind their overwhelming defeat, and left us nothing but their corpses.

Our casual attitude toward extinction has not extended to our cars.

Of course in the opera the aria came from, they would never sing like this, blinking in a casket, which would also never be white, a color held to be cold and without comfort.

Blue, yellow-green, brown and gray
bouree: so rapid motion imitates stillness

intermittent motion chisels a rounded edge

they call "by memory" "by heart," but only in certain situations

Nonviolence has become a conscious strategy. Even small children do not bat an eye.

Because I liked her I did not mind her feeling strongly about some things, and came to know and anticipate the objects of her aversion.

So the children were striving at recess   as she said   emily
who art thou   when you are blameless   and innocent of any
future   in men and insects' eyes

Enormous engravings of European faces rise and fall as back-drops, although the singers and dancers are often hidden behind them. All of these eyes manage to be closed while being open (through their expression) and are part of larger profiles that tell us nothing more. You point your toe into the floor as part of a long tradition of labor without purpose, the ballet.

It is only more of the same, but none the less valuable for it.

They imagine a future in which a continuous context would be something difficult to imagine.

For a long time now, engaged in the observation of lush spectacle, they are pleased to watch and listen to a story they do not understand.

They create a world in which the human scale is small, smallest in the manmade world.

Altogether they are powerful, although each one is small.

The spear makes bubbles.

Is it only the scale that has made the city monstrous?

I dreamt the weapon made me small. Everyone paid attention to it instead of me, as if I were carrying a baby.

They advance within the circle by redistributing their weight, but must sometimes rock to gain sufficient momentum. When they are vertical and oscillating, they seem to be courting.

Because of the rain, the summer days here have been dark. I left at the last minute. It was eleven at night: a thunderstorm put out the lights of the parking lot, shrouding it in darkness, in which lightning flared so suddenly and briefly that no one remembers seeing anything in its light but the pavement, white and textured, although memory tells us it is black. I tried to remember where my car was but this was impossible, since I never had understood where I put it, and I simply had to run around getting wet until I found it, trying not to run into other people doing the same thing.

A slight fluttering of panic, maroon, cerise, the seriousness of leisure.

I would have thought to see it struck would move me.

"A Distance Without Distance"

Through letters it's arranged to meet in Mexico. The immense city is more forbidding than ever, impossible even for those who cannot imagine living elsewhere. The intent is to use it only as a point of departure for somewhere else more manageable.

It must have happened on the way to the hotel or just after she arrived and was walking around the city to take it in while waiting for him. The street action she's swept up in began as an organized strike but in a time of so many strikes quickly loses definition, turning into a riot. The tense is uncertain: the changes that occur in the dream are like the flushes of color that pass through the skin of a dying fish or over the face of an enraged person. It was like a fire that sweeps people into hallways to escape it. She fled into a doorway to escape the street but in a time of so many people the street fled into the doorway and swept up the stairwell, pushing the people upward to avoid being trampled. Each person ran up the stairs to escape the crowd, but each person composed the crowd and crowded the other, in a rising spiral of panic. Each person was aware of composing the crowd, aware of the spiral they were assuming.

The stairs had been constructed for a leisurely survey of the city, and so each landing was of glass, commanding views more and more impressive. The ceiling of each level was progressively higher also, leading, she knew, to a final vaulted ceiling with a mural by a famous Mexican painter — *The Liberation of Labor*, an image of the present writhing in the past, a snake shedding its skin.

She began to conceive of where she was as the electricians' union, but this thought was pushed from behind by another, a memory of that building being elsewhere. It had been in a poor neighborhood with no tall buildings. The streets had deep holes, like the beginnings of caves (dogs rested in them), and pieces of broken machinery covered with dust. She found her way there while looking for the bead district. As the bodies surged forward, she saw that low building again — brick, rectangular, the calm proportions of an old theater. The seal on the gate, emblazoned with a lightning bolt and the name of the union, suddenly reminded her that she was definitively lost and must find her way back. She had asked several people for directions before getting an answer she could follow. A riot of images from her life with him, or her imagined life with him, flashed before her eyes, projected from behind as a movie is, absorbing her whole attention. She was beside herself. The times are mixed together, contaminated paragraphs, hybrid with something of the monstrous. She's beside herself, but aware of the stairway or landing walls on either side, plaster or glass, planes of peripheral blindness, blind spots shaped like wings.

The tide of people sweeps up toward the mural but then somehow, inexplicably, she's on the street alone, in front of his hotel.

Maybe it was her hotel, too, she couldn't remember, but before she could get her bearings she saw him, emerging from the narrow elevator surrounded by three or four other people. He looked thinner than she remembered, like an image of himself.

Although the disturbance she had been involved in had lasted for at least three days, that was the terror of the passage, that it could go on and on that way, up and up, all the way to the sky the way children say it, and with the feet of everyone having to keep moving, the way prisoners say they learn to march while sleeping, although the disturbance has lasted this long, he is happy and smiling.

He says he'd figured she was caught up in something. He wasn't worried but decided after a few hours to take advantage of an invitation to see some other places. He'd seen three countries and he said their names, but the only one she remembers is Paraguay.

Later all she remembers is being uncertain whether what has happened has already consumed their whole vacation, or whether some of it is left, and it can now begin.

When you've been driving for a long time at night you feel suddenly that you're traveling through nothing or that you're sitting still and the darkness is going past you, and that's how you know to pull over and stop.

But in a time of so much darkness it is fully inhabited so everything is lit, bright with people and buildings, and there is nothing to pull over into. An old cab pulled up, coughing like a horse, the driver's door stencilled in spray paint with the company name — AMPARO, and glancing at her he opened the door, spreading his gaze like a cloak and absorbing her whole attention.

What Happened Between Them
(The Departure)

1

She had met him without any introduction, part of a crowd that he was addressing. He spoke without reading from anything. She looked to see if he had any notes, but the podium prevented a view of his hands, which he raised up and brought together as he stepped back now and again, as if remembering something, his hands falling forward then while telling it, as if his ideas were something that had happened to him.

How could he talk to so many people as if he were addressing just one person? It made her feel she was understanding him in a way he had never been understood before. For she knew from his manner of presentation that he had given this same talk many times. Sometimes when he stepped back he almost seemed to be remembering those other occasions and then as he stepped forward to be remembering this one, as if it had already happened. But instead of this making him seem more distant, he seemed closer, as if she could feel exactly how she would be kept in mind, as if she were already with him in the future.

Therefore it seemed as if something had already happened between them, although they had not been introduced. In fact, thinking about it that way, she had not met him when she was part of the crowd but when someone introduced them. After that he sat a few rows behind her (still not really knowing her), and he became a part of the crowd and with her listened to other people talking. Later they talked about how they had heard all these other speakers, what they had thought and understood while listening to them, and felt they had heard them in almost the same way.

Maybe it was the next day or the day after (the conference was still going on) when she imagined she felt something extraordinary about him, as if he mattered a great deal to her. She was busy completing her work and preparing to leave the country and did not think any more about him until he called her one evening, just to say hello. Because she was in the northern part of the state and he in the southern, this seemed to indicate that he might have had a similar feeling.

She decided to go see him on the way to visit her parents, to say goodbye to them. He lived in a pleasant beach community, and she thought she might stay in the kind of motel she had often seen by the side of the road on her way across the country, shaped like a horseshoe with a swimming pool in the middle and a slide going into it, with no one swimming or sunbathing there. She imagined this motel by the sea, and thought it would give her a chance to rest. Working and packing up she had often gone without sleep. Driving out of the city for the last time, her car full of notes, gifts, and valuables, the sun was particularly hot for the spring, and she thought she could see it hit the hood and imagined the turquoise sheen turning as flat as poster paint, separating, flaking off. She was struck with how she was now doing something she had always wanted to do, to pack up all her things and depart.

Traveling in foreign countries easily turned her into another person. At first she was struck by how it turned her into no one. This was because she was still learning the language, and so when invited to meet an important person, took her friend with her and sat on the sofa, listening to the two men engaging in conversation. There was something relaxing about not having to be anybody, and when she went to the bathroom she spent a long time there, admiring a painting of children and kites in watercolors. There was no ground painted in: the children were standing on the paper, the sea was a waving line.

She came down the hill early in the morning to the outdoor market of Cumana. Awnings of the vendors made up an aisle of shade that looked even darker to her eyes, still used to the brilliant morning light coming down the hill. It was cool there in the darkness with the vegetables and fruit. As a piece of blue ice is dry and burns, you can read rain from clouds, and she began to be able to guess with increasing accuracy just how hot the day would be, as she stood there each time under the awnings, admiring the green oranges.

Usually solitary, it is not shy. Active at night, it remains motionless when alarmed. It feeds on fishes and insects.

They went after each other.

On the way back, going through the center, she spotted them from far away, three or four blocks that seemed like more because the streets were full of people and cars moving slowly and insistently around them, or the people moving around the cars. Their skin was a luminous black; they were very tall.

The cars in that town were not as terrifying as those in the city, older with oxidized paint that came off a little on her clothes as she brushed against a car waiting to turn while she threaded her way around it.

They ducked into a group taxi, holding onto their derby hats. They were speaking a beautiful language to the driver, trying to tell him where they wanted to go. They were English speakers, an English from the islands that sounds like singing. They were working on a boat and wanted the car to wait for them at the grocery store. By then she had learned the language and explained things to the driver before getting out.

It was bright again. A black car with a wreath of yellow and purple flowers moved in front of her. The other cars pressed through while she crossed. It was an image of patience, she thought, the herd of cars slowly moving forward while people walked in procession in the streets.

They are not shy. Small groups of them move back and forth, following the waves as they advance and running over the wet sand as they retreat.

She wrote home often so that the home would stay there. It was over the horizon, a thick blue strip of sea, the Caribbean. Cumana was a town of hills, so everything was close at hand. To see far away one walked uphill and looked. It was easy to move into any place seen in the distance except, of course, for the blue line that was the sea.

Before she met him she kept thinking about how things could be. It was a kind of daydreaming she'd been doing for as long as she could remember. Yet it wasn't something she remembered, but was like running her tongue over her teeth.

It was pleasant, like an extra room. It was fully prepared for her, because she could never quite make it out. It was like a place she could have always returned to, but because she had never been there, it was only an illuminated space.

It is shy; it makes mellow, rattling calls at twilight and builds a nest at the very top of the tree, a frail structure.

She was not sure which birds they were. It was getting dark, and in this light she was not even sure if they were blue or green. The two of them might be traveling together for just a little while, accompanying each other to the main flyway where they would lose their pair formation and join the flock, whose sound they begin to hear.

Or they might be parrots, the flock made up of pairs. Blue-headed parrots, with maroon faces and blue crowns. She had only seen the green kind in the darker green of the woods, in the wild, so that their greenness was not spectacular there. Only their flashes of yellow and red appeared brilliant as colors.

But she would find them through their sound. Those who imagined that the parrots talked (they said it sounded like singing) asked how they could talk to so many birds as if they were addressing just one, making individual but mutually understood sounds, bonding the mated pair.

Yet she had listened to them for a long time, making those sounds from the very tops of the trees. They never really answered each other, she thought. How they heard one another could only be speculation. That they could make spectacular mirrors of their voices while in captivity seemed to her to have given them an undeserved reputation.

While he was sleeping he was addressing a crowd of people. Through the walls of his dream and his closed but moving mouth she couldn't hear any of the words but understood the situation from the tone of his voice. He was taking pleasure in convincing them of something, exclaiming, his voice advancing out to them, then retreating into thinking out loud, still carrying them with him but then leaving them there with his thoughts and advancing all on his own to a conclusion they could not be complicit in, he having reached it ahead of them in a way indicating he had been there before, he had discovered it, this conclusion like a promontory or a spectacular canyon. Now he led them there, to see for themselves.

They tracked the animal without being sure of what it was into the thick green woods, where even their bright clothes were dark. It is surprising how close dark green can be to black. Yet there were frequent patches of light, and the sun so intense it appears to break the people into pieces as they travel along the path. The vine becomes part of the tree as it threads its way around it, and along it bromeliads and staghorn ferns have made their way, although the variety of roots and blossoms confuses them. The pale orchid first turns brown on the edge and then all of it where it falls, held by the roots until it disappears into something else entirely.

At first it had been wonderful to be kept in mind by him like that, steadily and closely, like something held or as if he were running his tongue over his teeth without noticing before speaking. He thought about her when she was not with him; he imagined being with her. She loved the way he was so absorbed in her, but was wary of his ideas of her, that they might eventually come to exist as a trap for her. She was someone for him, but part of her wanted to be no one while traveling. Now she enjoyed his being intent on her, but his gaze, strong as an arrow, might sometime strike her differently.

Groups of female red deer organize themselves around a system of protection: when they flee they assume the form of a spindle, with the leader in front and the second dominant individual in the rear. If they pass into a gully, the last individual will stop and fix the intruder with her eyes while the group disappears.

Although he had said they would remain friends, he no longer answered her letters, and when she spoke to him on the phone, his voice was cold and distant. She still had a sense of his body and felt his top lip coming down over the lower as he ended a sentence, and could see his forearms resting on the arms of his chair.

2

Because communication had been severed with him, she kept imagining that one day she would write something. It would be for him, but only secretly. His name would not be in it. None of his friends would be there, nor the town he lived in, nor his position. As she thought one by one of all the things she would be forced to eliminate about him, she felt a sudden sensation that might be called pain, but it was not pain. It was a kind of dislocation.

Imagine a place, inhabited. Then imagine that what has inhabited that place has been instantaneously removed and set down in another place. At the moment it is set down it has this sensation.

She felt this same sensation while running fast with her eyes to the ground, on suddenly looking up into the sky.

It's a pale blue sky, immense, with cirrus clouds, and they pull back into themselves again and again, very quickly, before they again release themselves, advancing. As this occurs they become even more dispersed, reconfiguring into a "mackerel sky," known in Venezuela as "the angel's wings."

The sensation occurs while the clouds retreat and advance and retreat and advance, over and over.

Meanwhile you know it's your own body playing tricks on you, making the whole scene change visibly, but only for you.

Someone else could not see it, someone else could not see it change, it would be still for someone else, although for you it is moving, moving until it stops.

In contrast, where he lived the sky was somehow "realistic" — a clean blue, matter-of-fact, often cloudless, or with clouds that had already achieved their shapes without us seeing them form, generous and reserved, their drift so slow and steady we perhaps only imagine it, as if it were a background to our thoughts, or an image of patience.

The beach where he lived had this same quality. There were cliffs, but there were also stairways. Blackbirds by the guardrails were blue, striking a note of ambivalence as they moved with sharp, back-and-forth motions, claws balancing on a surface of sand. Their feathers were purple, but a purple shifting off of the pure black as they moved, like an illustration of the theory of color.

This place still exists; I could go there again.

At first it was for him secretly to protect his privacy. While she thought of that she imagined his voice. She heard him talking to her casually about something, while he was still letting himself talk to her. At first his voice opened as that sky did: even on the phone she was conscious of his mouth opening while he spoke. Sometimes it opened into its own sound, so that he started to lose what he was saying. At first he took pleasure in that, that something of his own was being pulled away from him, he thought in her direction, and then it would always come back to him, sooner or later — sooner when they were first getting to know each other and then later, when being together created a place, inhabited.

He then handed her her clothes, without letting them get any sand on them. The sand had been almost hot, and had transferred its warmth to her skin, but standing up she saw that the clouds were now as strong as the sun. Her back was turned to him; she never thought about whether he was looking. She saw the wind lifting the blue water up in waves, now green and transparent, leaving a foam on the sand like salt. They had lost track of time and, chilled, moved back across the dunes in a hurry. Climbing up, the new wind pushed them and the sand rose up in waves, but over the top it was warm again. The sand was still hot there, resembling a location.

She said she had seen it happening in front of her, around her everywhere, "and I forgot it as it was happening." Now, years later, it came back to her and she was returning back to that place, just to know that it had occurred.

They did not necessarily say hello or goodbye to each other. Many people were living there, the whole village, and houses were shared. Sometimes they walked in to get something (a grater, shotgun, or radio) and threaded their way through the others there. When she asked him how they said goodbye, he answered *aduwa*, which means "now."

The film was based on returning to the places where these things had happened. I see what is now there, I listen to people who remember what happened, to people who have forgotten what happened, as well as to people who saw things without understanding them.

As he raised up his hands and brought them together, she was aware of his wrist and the way it moved. The fingers' gesture is not independent of the arm, and the wrist betrays this dependency, and is called delicate. Or the hand gestures, and the fingers of the hand do its bidding. But where did the bidding come from? The occupational therapist had thought for a long time about the origin of a simple gesture and how it could be made.

Hand: the terminal part of the arm. Ape hand: one with the thumb permanently extended, capable of grasping or seizing. While the human hand is capable of skillful motions, such as writing and sewing, made possible by the action of small muscles completely within the hand and of tendons of the arm muscles and by the coordination of nerve structures.

After a certain while the birds flew over and over, like clouds thoughtless in the sky. Or impelled, directed, whether by instinct or plan.

Something very important must be remembered. It is one's new name, the identity that must be assumed when dropped into Hungary. Although it is so important, it must not be written down, for if anyone were to see it, they would know immediately that something was wrong.

Some say that in order to remember it, they had to believe it was real, the way one shuts off familiar, intruding languages when speaking a new one. The men repeated their new names over and over to themselves, without moving their lips, until everything else disappeared.

Because it is all so vague, the proper names of countries appear brilliant as colors.

And I thought, as I was falling, I was asleep, I was this sensation of falling and of being set down. A tornado picks things up and puts them down this way. So does a giant. Wars do the same thing, or think of forced repatriation. Laws forbidding the use of a language. Forced collectivization. The denial of the right to privacy. Blind rage.

As I completed what I had written for you, I became aware of the words within it, as a person sitting quietly reading in a house at night may suddenly look up from the page and become aware of the house, its foundation, its beams and walls. Outside the sky was the deep blue called ink or midnight, what it achieves just before turning into black. All of the words were ones I had used before; I went over it carefully. There was no word in what I had written for you that I had not used before. I felt strangely comforted then, to think it was only a new arrangement, familiar words, neutral, in a new order.

After Fernand Léger's *Mural Painting*, 1926

(DE MENIL MUSEUM, HOUSTON)

I am not in agreement with the decisions you have made, made without making them, as if they would make themselves. They do not make themselves, and so I existed where they were not made. Suspended in oil, the pigments carry color as if with open hands, palms up, out asking.

The arms of the stylized mothers carrying their dead children as offerings in religious paintings also exist this way. All of their mourning has gone into their fingertips, cupping the head as if it were a flower. These are not the arms of the mothers who are fleeing along the roads of Asian countrysides in photographs, carrying children still living, asleep or awake, terrified, their eyes red, wild, as if painted in.

Oil has been this kind of vehicle of color for ages. It is not like the beeswax in this other painting from so many years later, taken and applied over alphabets. He chose to make them gray.

So I existed where other decisions were not made, among the forest of suspended decisions that might have been mine or someone else's. At last as in a dream I recognized them to be yours, and among columns of blue, green, and black, whose leaves were not stirring due to their enchantment with themselves, I touched the bark and opened the red door in the trunk.

The story was the painted surface of something else that both showed through and made it up. It came out then.

Holding One Another in Suspense
(After Paul Schrader's *The Comfort of Strangers*)

They were not with each other but circling around each other and in this way were holding one another in suspense. She kept a picture of her children in her purse and she asked him whether he liked children, and in this way she used the children to hold him off from her as she held the photograph away from her while she looked at it. She was not where the children were and she called the children with difficulty, and the calls did not reassure her but were merely used by her to create an idea of a home that was not with her, where they were. She could not then be at home if they were there, and if they were here where she was she could not really be with him, as she would be distracted.

He also circled around her, since he could not make up his mind if he really loved her or merely found her incredibly attractive. Thinking about this kept him from touching her, as when he touched her he felt he must know if he really loved her or was merely sleeping with her, but he did not know and so did not touch her. The tension of not touching her kept him from really concentrating and so he could not really think to make up his mind as to whether he really loved her and wanted to live with her.

They both liked to look at each other very much as each thought the other possessed a beautiful body but neither felt much pleasure in their own. It was necessary to care for the body and decorate it and this then appeared tedious to them. Yet they were always well dressed and appeared sexual although they never made love.

Seeing those who were cruel or who seemed estranged from them made them feel closer to each other and they began making love with each other. Yet while they were doing so each appeared as the children in the photograph had appeared, as if held out there at a distance being looked at.

What is pleasing gives no pleasure and there is no clue as to why this is so, only that something is missing in every place they go, and yet the thing that is missing cannot be obtained in another place and then brought back, for by the time they return the place will have changed and one other thing will be missing. This is like the story of the children from the southern hot countries who went to go get snow and brought it back in a truck where it first changed to water and then disappeared.

They seem to say that looking at something can never have as its object the understanding of the thing one is looking at, but merely that the eye derives pleasure from certain lovelinesses. Yet no pleasure is given and the eye merely registers certain lovelinesses. By inference we might know that the film is held before us like the photo of the children, images of people who are not here yet are speaking to us, not to each other but to us, knowing they are in a movie and getting sick sometimes from traveling but this not making it any more real.

What Makes Things Move

There is a difference between
what makes things move
and what stops them; it is what
moves things that arranges them.

— HÉLÈNE CIXOUS

1

Meanwhile, they kept waiting for the intensity to ease. They felt that they were making way for something, but they were not sure what it was. It appeared to be something historic, but they did not remember things that were historic seeming to be so personal before.

It reminded one of them of a movie she remembered seeing as a child, a western, where the town at various moments in the movie was shot from the same angle and height, that of a third-story apartment. People came through this town, which was more than an outpost but less than a proper town. She remembered the saloon, the general store, and the dusty roads that converged in front of these two places, which were equally elevated on their foundations and outlined by the banisters of their porches, so that three or four steps had to be climbed in order to come in.

There was a lot of movement in this film. People rolled into town to signature music, letting the audience know who the people were as the turning wheel of the stagecoach filled the whole frame, or a hand and forearm covered the screen, straining forward over the reins. Or there was a naked back against an open field and a big sky. There were the Indians, the cowboys, and the townspeople. And around them, like flames or falling leaves or things that crunched underfoot, were the women of the Indians or the townspeople. The cowboys had no women but one rescued a woman from the Indians by riding his horse very fast down the dusty road. His whole horse could be seen through the eye of the camera, galloping very fast amid the rhythmic sound and the neighing of the horse as it reared up on its hind legs while he picked the woman up and carried her off. He had to be quick about it, like a helicopter in another film she had seen that had picked up some prisoners from a Mexican prison to allow their escape, the whole trick of his coming into the town was to be there and gone almost before they knew it.

She must have seen that black-and-white film when she was very young, for she had practiced the scene with a friend of theirs over and over many times. Actually, it had been with her older sister, the same one that she had practiced getting married to many times, although neither would later stage this sort of wedding.

They had no horse and so one of them just had to go around the house where she (the older one) could not be seen. She was then to "gallop" at full speed into the patio, which was to be the space the elevated camera had captured, in front of the saloon and the general store. For them it was in front of the picture window through which dining room chairs can be barely made out in a black-and-white photograph she has recently found. The sun was bright that day; it was the fall. A huge fire-tree stood over the patio, like a remnant of a primordial forest, which had to be tied down during storms so that it did not fall on the bedroom of the girls.

The younger was to sit on the brick circle around the tree, pretending she was held by Indians who were for a moment absorbed in their own business while the older sister burst upon the patio. She saw her reflected in the window that the cool sun turned into a mirror, broken by a grid of white lines dividing the panes. The ropes restraining the branches above them were thick brown twisted hemp; the fire-tree's yellow and red blossoms are only black-and-white forms in the mirror of the picture window, so she knows she must be remembering through the photograph. They were both remembering, while her sister was grabbing her, the scene in the movie and the fascinating way the cowboy had picked up the woman, so strong and definite, as if her weight was not that of a person but of a mailbag that hung beside a train. (That was another movie of suddenly capturing something by taking it in one clean motion, shot with the camera held out the window by a passenger inside the train as it approached the hanging mailbag that was then scooped up, with the mailbag itself cut into the next frame that had no train in it and no mail, so that its gray canvas was a final destination or death of all the accelerating movement toward it.)

They could never do this scene right (that was why they did it over and over) because to sustain the intensity she must be lifted up with no resistance and run away with as if without effort, as if recovering something that already belongs to you as definitely as your own body. Her sister was only two years older and could not manage it.

2

The civilization of the Indians was in danger, although in the movie they did not call it a civilization but "our tribe." This was another game they played, and it was always better to be a murderer than the one that got killed, although there was one child from down the block, an odd boy with curly hair, who always insisted on being the one that got killed and loved to scream.

Because the civilization of the Indians was in danger the cowboys could not be allowed to stage their genocide, even though the woman held by the Indians was in danger of unspecified tortures. The townspeople, who sometimes also rode horses and so might be thought of as good cowboys, except that they had women, could achieve justice while allowing the Indians to live. They thought only that the Indians must go away a little, move a little further away from the settlement that was becoming a town. (The women did not have to move away, although many were still in the East, not yet being frontier women, who in this movie mostly stayed inside the houses making up the backdrop for the groups of people rolling into town.) The townspeople could achieve justice through the law, but first they must do away with the bad cowboys, who have tight aggressive bodies with arms pushing against the fabric of their long sleeves, riding into town. They have powerful thighs, and their horses have powerful muscles that ripple under their shining coats.

At the fateful moment when the cowboys rode into town to massacre the Indians holding the woman the camera was held at the level of the ground, directly facing the horses that came riding, came galloping in, so that as the cowboys neared, more and more of the horses rather than the cowboys could be seen, hooves violently kicking up dust that finally blurred the picture, just as the camera had disappeared into the gray canvas mailbag in the other movie.

But just as in that other movie, at that moment one saw the good cowboy riding in to rescue the woman who was now the girl sitting on the brick circle under the fire-tree, about to feel the awkwardness of her body as she tried to turn it into a kind of package that could be picked up with the same grace the cowboy had displayed in the film, but which in fact although smaller than the woman's was too heavy for her sister, who staggered and ruined the effect.

3

Yes, while they were waiting for the intensity to ease, as if they were making way for something that might be historic, she felt that sensation that had occurred for her watching that film, just at the moment when the camera captured an equal portion of cowboys and their horses, before the flanks of the animals bore down.

4

And there was not any easing of the intensity, of the tension, just as there had not been in that film, not for him anymore than for her. For at the moment that the actress was swept up, the mailbag was seized, and the camera was pulled out from under the hooves of the furious horses, at that moment in which they were waiting, a new twist in the plot overtook them, not giving them a moment's rest. If they had been waiting for one parent to die for a long time, nursing that parent, the other parent would die suddenly, but only after giving one a terrible message. Or as one of them was about to complete a novel about a new republic that is invaded, thieves would enter her apartment, and she would lose everything that belonged to her. Or the tiny birds nesting just outside who were about to fly for the first time would be startled as the tree that their parents had selected, which had in fact been dead for some time, would fall over, pushing them into the air involuntarily.

And what happened then, in that moment they had chosen and dreamed of entering, but not quite now, not just yet, not with no ground under their feet, what happened then?

5

Although in the narrow channel the large vessel normally makes way for the small vessel, it is not required to do so. Neither is the situation governed by whether one is under power or under sail. It is more a matter of vectors, laid down on the legal map as if they are sticks, something having to do with entering or leaving the harbor, she found out a long time ago and does not exactly remember. She found out by climbing up more than three or four white wooden steps, to come in to the harbormaster's station, shortly after being rammed or, as the owner of the yacht claimed, ramming. The owner of the yacht was already out to sea and did not care. His size left him unscathed.

6

This shows that to make way for something, even if it is an unknown thing, requires a certain attentiveness to what is coming, a certain respect for it or concern that it be made way for. If instead one is merely lounging on the deck of one's vessel, one is either run over by what is coming or one is struck, injured to an extent freely ranging from the mortal blow to the slightest dent, or one may be ignorant completely of something having come at one that could have been made way for, observed or greeted or met. It depends on size.

7

The dictionary says that a western is a film set in the latter half of the nineteenth century, but she remembers traveling through the West and seeing ghost towns that looked a lot like the town in that movie she remembered.

He wrote that "behind the splendor of great capitals I enjoy detecting a ghost town struggling to be released . . ."

The ghost town would push against the splendor as the arms of the cowboys pushed against the fabric of their long sleeves.

While she lived near Hollywood there was a scandal because a helicopter in a staged war had to repeat an incident over and over many times, the director having an exact idea of what he wanted. During the last take there was a bad accident in which several actors were killed, including a child she imagines remembering was Vietnamese. They may have been working too long, for too many hours, or this may have taken place at dusk, with inadequate lighting.

Actually, the problem had been that they were filming a rescue operation, the shot taking place at that intense moment when the war was about to end and the Communists come in, and this rescue was imagined by the director to require the helicopter to fly lower than permitted by regulation. Although the actors objected, the director insisted, and they were killed, although the director may have been killed also, she found out a long time ago and does not exactly remember.

"Siempre quise crear lo real"
("I Always Wanted to Create the Real" — Alfredo Chacon)

1

In the city where she lives, people give directions by saying *subiendo*, "going up," or *bajando*, "coming down," meaning toward or away from the mountain. Caracas is situated alongside this range that rises to nine thousand feet high, The Avila. Trees march down it into the city, grand even next to buildings of ten or twenty stories. By regulation they cannot be cut down, or must be transplanted in exactly their original relation to the sun.

Green mountains can be seen from her bedroom eight floors up, filling the window frame, horizon obscured by a long cloud moving steadily right to left, east to west. "If you climb over the mountain you'll find the sea."

She said that lying in bed with him, wondering if she could still daydream about his body if he was here. He was here, to the right of her and over her, with no clothes on next to her. She was naked too, lying on her back under the weight of his arm, his chest still leaning against her, as if pressing her into the bed. The moment was about to pass, and she was probably about to tell him another story.

•

The last time she daydreamed about his body was by the sea, the one on the other side of the mountain. It had been a nice daydream right after swimming, lying on her stomach in the sand, skin still excited by its contact with the salt and currents of the Caribbean. It was a beautiful day, sunny, she could hear people walking along the shore or running shouting into the waves. Her physical position, the towel placed where the incline of the undertow began (she liked the sand well packed down), seemed to connect her to their conversations, although she couldn't hear what they were saying. That was alright, her thoughts were softening like crayons in the sun that became him, bearing down on her.

•

He has lifted himself off of her, as if waking up, rolling over so as to sit up slowly, as if telling her that there is no division between where they were ten minutes ago and where they are now. He's looking out the window. If two forms of perspective are used in a painting, do they cancel each other out? His ankles are crossed and he's naked on the bed, smoking.

•

"It has a very strange atmospheric surface and the image is of a woman wearing a hat."

•

They felt themselves at an advantage or a disadvantage to the day as they went outside, walking through the revolving door of the hotel. If you think of their room as separate from the day they are starting the day late, since they were there all morning. A large square is in front of the hotel. In the cool air the scents of formal gardens on either side of the road in front of them are distinct as their going out the door.

If you think of their room as part of the day they have started the day more or less at the same time that most other people have and are now going out to join them.

.

He was thinking about the multiple openings of her body as he examined the canvas to see how the paint was laid down.

.

The image of the sea was an etching, incised and then printed. In some places she further colored it with the tip of a very fine brush, watching as she did so what was already there. She had made the incising, and another had printed it, so that as she painted it her hand responded to its own previous movements, and to the qualities of the metal plate, the ink, and the paper.

It made an image of points of light on water shifting in their nature from the direct to the once-removed hand. There is no horizon line. So I thought that we must be looking down, but the image made it clear that we were not looking at the sea, but at points of green and black ink on paper. Or this was like a formal portrait of the sea, where the sea could sit precisely so we could see it. The green was that color that is named for the sea, not bottle or celery green but sea green, a color that is often a clue to the temperature of the water.

.

Although it is surprising how close dark green can be to black, all small distinctions were registered here, plain to see.

.

As the color of the firmament depends on the coming together and the nature of the opaque vapors suspended in the air, we do not marvel that the sky seen over Venezuela's vast wilderness is of a blue darker than the depths of the sea. An air hot and nearly saturated with humidity is continually floating up from the surface of the sea to the highest regions of the atmosphere, where a very cold temperature reigns. This ascending current creates a precipitation or, more accurately, a condensation of vapors, in times when clouds are never seen, in the driest air that rests over continents; or they stay apart, suspended in an atmosphere whose color is then pale. From the heights of the Andes a haze extends, covering the surface of the ocean like a

light, even veil. Yet when one is at sea this same air appears per-
fectly pure and transparent, and the existence of these opaque
vapors is hidden from sailors by the intense blue of the sky.

.

He was not really thinking about the multiple openings of her
body but certain of his movements remembered themselves. As
he reached out to close the door he remembered her with her
back to him, his hand reaching out for her right shoulder, and
pulling it toward him it was her.

Or as a woman looked at him in the street and their eyes met he
remembered her mouth uncertain for a moment around the
level of his belt and then, her hands pulling his clothing toward
his feet, closing over him.

It was a wonderful kind of work she was doing, but he was not
thinking this while her mouth was working over him, only feel-
ing the exact sensations of her tongue and teeth, forgetting he
was inside her, or whose sensations they were.

The colors were pink and white, soft but unsentimental, the
breast feathers of a bird; or they were in the dark, or it was get-
ting dark, or the light was yellow. Because it had been at differ-
ent times of the day that they had been in bed together. He
remembered that when it got dark he noticed that the light did
not leave the room but the darkness entered it, saturating the
light with its multiple points of darkness.

•

On a number of occasions we have recorded the orientation of the beds composing this vast range by the sea as being from the north to the southeast, with the inclination ordinarily northeast. So the orientation of those that were first laid down is independent from that of the range today. This may be noted from Puerto Cabello to Manicuare and Macanao. On the island of Margarita one finds granite from west to east, then to the right of it gneiss, over it micalike slate and primitive slate, next to a final bed of gypsum and agglomerates containing shells from the open sea.

•

It was the desire to return, to return to what she had left, knowing that what was behind her was already changing, but perhaps because of that wanting to return, before it was transformed beyond recognition.

She wants him, she pulls him toward her, she comes toward him, she advances.

Without looking she felt his hands on her thighs. Both of his hands were there.

She imagines him desiring her in the same way she once wrote about young boys turning into men. This was when she was a young girl, turning into a woman.

She had one of those mouths that when closed appears to be withholding its words, actively, like a line struggling with itself to become what it already is but does not yet accept.

So she resisted for a moment before she lifted her hips toward him and arching her back, closing her eyes, looked for his hand with hers and pressed it further into her.

•

With the disappearance of the landscape, artists such as Alejandro Otero, Carlos Cruz-Diez, and Jesus Soto have taken from nature the principle of internal movement . . .

•

Pressing him further into her, she reached out for his other hand and held it, the tension of these hands then working as a measurement of something that is happening.

•

During the Middle Ages, these scenes took place in the open air, hardly ever happening inside before the fifteenth century, at which time they become common: *Love scenes and conversations are henceforth set in the enclosed space of a room.*

When martial law was declared, people had to stay inside for three days. After these days passed, they were allowed to go out until seven o'clock in the evening, and then after a month, they returned to their habits of old.

.

On the day of the census, people were commanded to stay indoors. Outside, the usual morning traffic noise was absent, and in its place were other sounds that had been there before without being heard. These were the sounds of animals and birds and the sounds of doors opening and being closed, of something with hinges being shut, of someone picking something up and putting it down.

.

And she said, "I'm not telling you about something that has already happened. I'm in something and I'm telling you about it while it's going on."

.

The cloud, as big as the mountain, is white, and struggling through it, the sky, in pieces of independent color. A dark and serious sapphire blue. An aquamarine, as if reflecting not the city but a northern sea. A baby or eggshell blue, almost as pale as the white running through it.

That white is the sunlight behind it or the threads of the cloud in front of it.

Because when you look at the sky as if it were a painting, a sun is shining through it or there are clouds in front of it. But shining through what, in front of what? No, it is real: the sun and the clouds are in the sky and make it up.

·

And I saw I had been holding off from my own life, holding it off from me. Yes, I had my arms up in this posture of defense. At first I was only conscious of my arms, stiff and aching as if I had been holding them up all night, a little like the sensation of my body after the accident. Then I became aware of pushing something away, and even while pushing it away, it was warm and attractive, like the body of another person. But it is my own body I thought as the tension released itself in a sudden escape, potent but fast and vaporous, like a sudden escape of steam.

·

The space between these multiple points of darkness was the space between the particles of his body after he left her standing in the doorway. At first he had waited for the band of youths to pass, the electric light of the outdoor entryway seeming an open enclosure. Something inside him had shattered without any violence, and everything seemed like an open enclosure, even his own skin. He realized it was permeable, his body exquisitely light. As he had been in bed before, he was listening to everything his body was doing and accepting it. Now he was walking down the street in the last part of the night that remained, the absence of traffic another opening, allowing him to enter it unimpeded until a car appeared. It paused for him as he crossed, as if in agreement with him, in agreement with his body, an animate car made of metal that could undergo stress at high altitudes but was safe here on the ground.

.

No reinforcements are needed.

.

The child thought for a long time about where the sky began. It wasn't down here on the ground, but it didn't begin anywhere. This was a problem she encountered while drawing, where to begin coloring in the sky. This could be solved, the teacher said, by making a horizon line.

.

The children breathe the air more or less three feet lower than we are breathing, and as contaminated substances are heavier than the free air of the atmosphere, they remain closer to the ground and therefore closer to the children; in the last few years in Caracas there has been an enormous increase in cancer in dogs and cats, who breathe at the height of our children.

.

She remembered being in that hospital room the first night with her tiny daughter who had begun shutting down, one by one, expressions of herself and her "vital signs," in order to conserve her life.

They must concentrate on themselves in this way.

Therefore when a very young child recovers from being seriously ill they will be seen to be going backwards. If before they had been able to say about twenty words they will now be back to "mama" and "up," for example, or if they had been walking well and beginning to run they now will be learning to walk again, swaying a little while they are moving forward.

.

And when the cloud moves off the mountain, it always moves down, down into the city. It comes down from the mountain, something big and white that walks into the city like a fragment of the night. The mountain stays there, like an idea that the city had during the night. A big idea, as big as the city.

Looking at the sky as if it were a painting you can't think about yourself in space, as part of the picture, and you can't imagine yourself acting like this.

You can't picture yourself that way.

But sometimes people are pictured that way, as angels.

2

And when I arrived there, in that village on the Hudson so close to Manhattan, I was struck by how the surrounding parkland had preserved a sense of the ongoing life of animals and birds, of trees, berries, and bushes, of what is not human, so that against the sounds of the traffic the sounds of the birds vied.

Yet it was clear which side would be making accommodations.

.

He wrote that sixty years ago Manhattan was nothing more than a campsite overlooking hundreds of corrals. At some time this may have been true, but not sixty years ago. That's why he puts that number in there, to make it sound accurate and inaccurate at the same time.

His precise location is between things. He's got to keep moving.

It took him more than three years to stop thinking of himself as between jobs when he went to work for himself.

The things he is between are also moving.

He's the man responsible for the final discrediting of the term "abstract painting" (see the landmark essay, "What Are Real Objects in Nature?").

He finds his attention captured by the blurring of what is fully articulated.

•

They like to talk about how Manhattan was traded for jewelry.

Manhattan and Caracas are both Indian names. We took them, trading the use of these names for the extinction of the original inhabitants.

•

The geographical position of Caracas can have a dark and severe aspect, particularly during that part of the year when the temperature is coolest, in November and December. The mornings then are of great beauty. In a sky that is pure and serene shine the two rounded pyramids of the Silla and the toothy crest of the Cerro de Avila; later in the afternoon the atmosphere is heavier, the mountains blurred over. Streams of vapor can be seen suspended above the always-green slopes, dividing the mountain into zones which, little by little, are confused, and the cold air descending from the Silla arrives in the valley and condenses in light vapors or large tufted clouds.

But this aspect that is so sober and melancholy, this contrast between the serenity of the morning and the clouded sky of the afternoon, is not observed in the summer. The nights of June

and July are clear and delicious, and the atmosphere is one of
nearly uninterrupted transparency.

.

It was July and Manhattan was deserted. You could cross the
street without looking and park anywhere.

While crossing you can even look up the street and see a car not
bearing down on you but half a block away, just heading your
way. Because of the space between you and the car, you can
even notice what kind it is and consider waving.

.

She stayed in that place long enough to see a little of what it
would be like to live in that neighborhood. She began to know
those men who lived outside, on the street, their habits. They
weren't like the other people one encountered there, who just
happened to be passing by while you were passing by. They
lived there, and not being on their way to anywhere they spent a
long time shifting where they sat, or getting up and sitting
down, or moving in patterns whose regularity could be estab-
lished, like the light of another apartment that comes on and
goes off at the same time every day. One would sit with his back
against the wall, staring at his shoes, while another would
weave down the sidewalk holding himself off from staggering,
moving forward while swaying a little toward the image of

himself as a sober man. It had not entirely left him. Another often stood on the corner, proclaiming.

Looking down from that loft where she was staying she later saw his upturned face, calling not to people, as she had thought, but to the sky. His eyes were vacant, but his voice spiralled upward in a high, practiced tone, traveling to heaven. Like his body, it was being used or inhabited. But when the shouts hit the gray space around the level of her window, they stopped being vehicles or arrows and disappeared.

When Humboldt climbed up there, there were people living there, gardens, bananas where today there is only savannah. It's the same today north of there, in Galipan. I've heard they want to get people out of there, to make it a national park, but those people know how to live there without making that place disappear.

•

An unpopulated country presents itself to the European as a city abandoned by its inhabitants. When one has lived in America for a number of years in the jungles and at the foot of mountain ranges, and when one has seen countries as extensive as France which do not contain even basic cottages, one's imagination is no longer frightened by the vast solitude. One accustoms oneself to the idea of a world that cannot exist apart from its plants and animals, where wilds exist that have never heard shouts of joy or the miserable accents of pain.

•

When she first arrived she had seen people using onramps as exits to the freeway, here called a highway, punctuated with stoplights once it hits midtown.

This would never happen on the West Coast, but before she left that place she did the same thing, seeing ahead of her a line of cars that meant a two-hour wait. There was a stream of cars doing the same thing as her, and they looked to each other as they moved onto surface streets to see if anyone knew another way, but no one did.

•

Due to movements of the earth, one hundred and fifty bridges in Venezuela are on the verge of collapse.

•

"If you climb over the mountain you'll find the sea."

These words, wandering out of her mouth, betrayed her. Or they would have betrayed her in her own country, where she sometimes wanted to eat her words, thinking she'd said them just for the sound of them, not really meaning them, as when she used the word "glory" one day and met with disapproval.

But here the sounds of things appeared used to meaning something. Others clearly were enjoying the music too, and might throw her way some words that were not entirely theirs either. So these words did not betray her here, in this city where looks are continuous, moving over a stranger's body like a hand, then moving on. They came out and flew around for the time it took to say them.

A man had driven down the mountain to sell vegetables off his truck. And when a woman this morning got mad at having to wait to pay him while he struggled to pull beets, carrots, lettuce off large mounds surrounding him, with people coming up and calling out with what they wanted, when that woman began denouncing him, calling him "a tiger," they saw she was crazy but her language fit. She was part of the morning, the truck by the tree in its shade, the soft shadow of the early day, the dirt on the beets and the spinach the way it grows in warm countries, as if on the verge of bolting.

.

"The sun came out."

It began to seem natural to her that her own voice was made up of observations, some of which were being made while she was using it.

The white of the cloud won't suffer comparison to anything. Paper's white, snow's white, the aymada fish in the southern rivers here is white, but the white of the cloud is the white of the sun without being the sun.

•

It's not a body, but it moves like one. It is a vapor. Yet it staggers, breaking its solidity and turning into patches of mist. It's a body of vapors revealed where its density decreases, and you see a bunch of threads hanging there.

If the cloud is as big as the mountain, it hides the mountain. When it's that big it hides the sky, as the darkness leaves. The darkness leaves without knowing if it is the day or the night it is leaving because it is becoming light as it is leaving, and is as uncertain as the cloud.

Leaves without knowing anything.

•

We see it as a surface because we are not angels.

The jewels that were originally rocks are still rocks but cut up to display themselves.

This is no more surprising than the sky appearing to be infinite, or being infinite.

•

He was talking about his life and how he hovered over it as if it were a painting he was looking at, as if it were a surface.

•

I thought that I'd like to bend over you.

•

Crossing the room in front of him. He will remain lying on the bed for a few moments while she gets up and crosses the room in front of him.

•

You could approach him without him seeing you and then you could watch him registering your approach.

If he saw you first, as when you met him at the airport, you would instead hear him calling out your name, looking for where the sound came from, and you could find him there, waiting for you.

•

When the chief came into the room we were using as a kitchen, he saw the amaryllis I had gathered in a vase. (It was a mineral-water bottle, clear glass stamped with green and yellow, left by the Catholic missionary thirty years before.) He looked at the flowers with concentration. I saw it was the first time he had seen this done. Then he said, in a gentle and tolerant tone, "Why?"

•

When the windows are open and the night breeze blows the curtains around, sucks them back, fills them again, is it just air coming in, the air of the night, night in the city, in the city that contracts even as it expands into garish flowering dreams, those figures for cakes, the Virgin, numbers, Disney characters made of sugar, coated with icing stiff as cement?

•

The disposition of his body is like a language. He sleeps like a baby. He fights off sleep, curling up, as if he is on a bench. He holds off the memory of other voices, now actually dead, that once talked to us in person about how real people become ghosts.

•

He wrestled with sleep like a man reading a strong sentence.

•

As she walked into the bathroom to wash, she envisioned him as an odalisque, but only in the position of his body. It was just an image that she had been given, a memory of soft curves and smooth skin now evoked by him. It did not include her thinking of him as a slave in a harem, perhaps because he was not looking at her, but off into space.

She saw him as free to look there, as not having to think of her looking at him, and so was glad she could not see his face.

•

One day, from my mother's bed, I saw a sleeping bat hanging from the ceiling, its head upside down. Suddenly it began to flutter above me. I had the sensation that this animal had two heads and was flying in pursuit of its own shadow. Now I realize that at that moment I noticed the existence of the spaces between objects, became aware of perspective, and from then on was conscious of being present, here, on the earth.

•

Now the situation of Caracas is very special, for it is situated at the foot of a mountain seven to nine thousand feet high. So there are not only geographic winds corresponding to the latitude of the city, but also the local winds of the mountain. In the day, the sun is strong, heating up the whole city; when the

night falls this heat releases itself in a sudden escape, and the
air rises in a perpendicular fashion. This process presents us
with a zone of less atmospheric pressure in the city, "sucking"
the air down from the mountain, so that each night the cool air
of the mountain comes down to the city, working as the vast
lung of Caracas.

•

Because of all the buildings, only part of the sun's ascension
could be seen. Between the level of the horizon and the skyline
it remained hidden. Hardly anyone even thought that it was
making everything light. The night just turned into the day.

•

Daydreaming about his body, she could never quite make it out.
Some room, somewhere, in a yellow light . . . It was like a place
that she could have always returned to, but now that we are
here, we no longer need to return. She could not still daydream
about his body if he was there. She no longer imagined him; she
grasped his real body, she held him to her.

So she "gave up the ghost," an antique phrase used for dying.

Are these the circumstances in which mirrors were formerly
covered?

•

Just after her child's birth, on the mother's first walk outside in the snow, she sighted a flock of green parakeets that had alighted on a pine tree whose needles were hidden by snow. They are the descendants of escaped birds who banded together and manage to live as far north as Boston.

•

Standing in front of the paintings a long time, reading things into the shapes.

Prints or the tracks of deer, tennis shoes.

An unknown history.

The dying green leaves turn brown, gray, silver and white. Stopping after walking for a long time there, the white, gray, and brown branches retreated into the pale blue sky.

What is it he means when he writes that despair has no face?

•

Hardly anyone even thought that it was making everything light.

•

They came out and flew around for the time it took to say them.

•

I don't want to have to make things happen to them. It seems to me a form of violence. Even if these things are "good," the forcefulness of my making them happen precludes other possibilities. So I waited for the events to arrange themselves easily. I waited for the events to communicate their nature to one another and, as a body, to find their natural conclusion.

NOTES

After Christoph Hein's *The Distant Lover*

Italics quoted directly from *The Distant Lover* by Christoph Hein, translated from the German by Krishna Winston and published by Pantheon Books, New York, 1989.

"Siempre quise crear lo real"
("I Always Wanted to Create the Real" —Alfredo Chacon)

Title quoted from *El Nacional* interview with Alfredo Chacon, Venezuelan cultural-historian-turned-poet, who gave this answer when asked why he turned.

Italics: pp. 103-5, 112-14, and 120-21 translated by the author from a Spanish version of Alexander von Humboldt's chronicle of his 1799–1804 travels in South America; p. 119: Robert Duncan, "The Structure of Rime I"; p. 120: translated by the author from Fernando Ortiz's series of interviews with Wifredo Lam, Havana 1950.